THE UNUSUAL LATKE PARTY

A Collection of Nontraditional Latke Recipes

Yuning Wang Pathman

Copyright © 2019 by Yuning Wang Pathman
All rights reserved.
No portion of this book may be reproduced or transmitted in any form without prior permission.

Published by Mauruuru Publishing House

Text, recipes, photography, styling, and design by Yuning Wang Pathman
Editing by Jeff Pathman

ISBN: 978-0-578-60931-7

DEDICATION

This book is dedicated to my parents, who cultivated an ardent curiosity about other cultures and a deep passion for experimentation in me, and to my husband for his love, inspiration, support, and encouragement that I can always count on.

And to all our regular Unusual Latke Party guests – our close families and friends, our AEPi brothers from Cal-Poly SLO and their families, our Honeymoon Israel family, and our Congregation Beth Jacob family.

TABLE OF CONTENTS

- ACKNOWLEDGEMENTS ... ii
- INTRODUCTION ... iii
- CHAPTER 1   CLASSIC POTATO LATKE RECIPE AND TIPS ... 1
  - CLASSIC POTATO LATKE RECIPE ... 1
  - LATKE MAKING TIPS ... 2
  - THE ELECTRIC DEEP FRYER – A HANUKKAH MIRACLE ... 4
- CHAPTER 2   THE UNUSUAL LATKE RECIPES ... 5
  - BAAA-LAPEÑO LATKE ... 7
  - BAKED BRIE LATKE ... 9
  - BUTTERNUT SQUASH AND WINTER SPICE LATKE ... 11
  - CAPRESE LATKE ... 13
  - COCONUT SWEET POTATO LATKE ... 15
  - COCONUT S'MORES LATKE ... 15
  - DEEP FRIED BANANA LATKE ... 17
  - HAGGIS LATKE ... 19
  - HONEY WALNUT SEA BASS LATKE ... 21
  - LOTUS ROOT AND GINGER LATKE ... 23
  - PAD THAI LATKE ... 25
  - PEKING DUCK LATKE ... 27
  - SILKY TARO LATKE ... 29
  - STICKY RICE FLOUR LATKE ... 31
  - SUSHI LATKE ... 33
  - THAI CURRY LATKE ... 35
- BONUS RECIPES ... 37
  - MEATZABALLS, CHEETZABALLS, AND PIZZABALLS ... 37
  - SCHLACHT-FUDGE ... 44

ACKNOWLEDGEMENTS

I want to start by thanking my husband and my mother for their support in the making of this book. Lots of work goes into it, from recipe testing to photography, from writing to proof reading… Without them, this book would not have been possible.

Thank you, Dad, for letting me have your awesome Canon camera set. You will be happy to know I put it to good use.

A very special thanks to Matt Schlachtman who contributed the Silky Taro Latke recipe and the Schlacht-fudge recipe. Schlacht-fudge has become THE dessert of our parties. Matt is probably one of the most creative people I know.

Also, a special thanks goes to Amanda and Jeremy Fox who contributed the Baaa-Lapeño Latke recipe. This recipe is one of my absolute favorites over the years.

Thanks to Cole Fox for his inspiration and advice on self-publishing a recipe book.

I also want to thank my mother-in-law, Michelle, who taught me how to throw a great party.

INTRODUCTION

When Jeff and I first started dating, Jeff would cook and invite me over for dinner. Around Jewish holidays, he would make traditional Jewish holiday food. These date night dinners were my first encounters with latkes. Due to the time constraints (cooking after work) and the limited cooking skills of a 24-year-old bachelor, they were made from Manischewitz box mix. Yet they were hot, creamy, full of flavor, cooked perfectly golden brown and filled with love. I fell in love with Jeff, as well as latkes. We would make latkes for Hanukkah every year, not from box mix, but from scratch. From time to time, we would try to add new flares to the age-old recipe. The results were mixed, sometimes good, sometimes bad. But regardless they were fun. In fact, we had so much fun creating it, after we got married and bought our first house, we decided to throw an Unusual Latke Party. Here's our party invitation:

"'Tis the season to temporarily get off the low fat/low carb diet and consume a lot of fried potato pancakes. This year we challenge you to take latke making to the next level - find/create/experiment with new latke recipes and share with everybody. For example, Yuning is thinking about Beef Latkes (not hamburger patties), Sweet Potato and Apple Latkes, Sushi Inspired Latkes, ...

So if you feel like taking up the challenge, please bring an unusual latke dish to share. If not, a degreaser such as a green salad, a fruit salad, or beer is always welcomed..."

Just like that, it became a tradition. We've been hosting it for 5 years now. The different ingredients not only added extra flavor and color to the traditional Hanukkah staple, but also brought breadth and depth to the holiday celebration by blending different cultures.

Over the years, we collected some recipes that are definite winners. I want to share them with everyone. Hopefully this book sparks your creative spirit. Please share what you have come up with.

Chag sameach and bon appetit!

CHAPTER 1 – CLASSIC POTATO LATKE RECIPE AND TIPS

CLASSIC POTATO LATKE

Makes 36 2" mini latkes

2 lbs potatoes, peeled	1 cup all-purpose flour	2 tsp table salt	(Optional) Sour cream
2 medium size onions	2 tsp baking powder	1 tsp black pepper	(Optional) Apple sauce
3 large eggs, beaten		Oil for frying	

1. Hand grate potatoes with a box grater or use a food processor with a coarse grating disk to grate the potatoes and the onions. If using a food processor, quickly chop the potatoes with a chopper blade for a few seconds before feeding them through the grater disk. Wring out as much liquid in the mixture as you can with a cheese cloth. If not used immediately, soak the shredded potatoes in water. *See Latke Making Tips #1 through #4 on Page 2 and Page 3*
2. Combine all dry ingredients (flour, salt, baking powder, black pepper) and mix well. *See Latke Making Tip #6 on Page 3*
3. Slowly pour in beaten eggs. Mix as you pour in the eggs. Stop adding eggs as soon as all ingredients are well bound and can form a lump. *See Latke Making Tip #6 on Page 3*
4. Put a heaping spoonful of potato mixture into your hands and form patties.
5. Pour oil into an electric deep fryer and heat to 360°F. Drop the latke patties into the hot oil and fry for about 2 minutes or until golden brown. *See Latke Making Tip #8 on Page 3*
   If you are using a frying pan, pour oil into the pan (about 1/4" high). Heat oil. Drop a few heaping spoonfuls of potato mixture into hot oil and flatten with a spatula. Fry for about 3 minutes or until golden brown. Flip over and fry the other side for about 2 minutes or until golden brown.
6. Serve hot with sour cream and/or apple sauce.

LATKE MAKING TIPS

1. Many stories are told, including "Nothing is like the latkes Bubbe used to make. Her secret is to hand-grate all the potatoes." Chances are the magic is in something else she did, and not in the manual grating process. There is very little difference between hand-grating and food processor grating, except that hand grated potatoes are thinner and shorter, which gives the latkes a creamer texture. However, when you are trying to make latkes for 30 people, hand-grating is not an option. BUT, there's a trick: Run the potatoes through the food chopper attachment for a few seconds (or hand chop the potatoes into smaller chunks) then run coarsely chopped potatoes through the grating disk. If you run whole potatoes through the grating disk directly, it tends to come out too thick and stiff. Your latkes will end up looking like hash browns.

See the pictures on the left. The plate at the top left shows how hand grated potatoes look. They are very thin, short, and appear to be juicy and lumpy. The plate at the bottom contains food processor grated whole potatoes. They are thicker and longer. The finished product will look and taste more like hash browns. The plate at the top right displays potatoes that were chopped in a food processor first, and then shredded with a food processor grating disk. They closely resemble hand-grated potatoes to their left.

2. Do not expose shredded potatoes to oxygen for more than a few minutes. They will be oxidized and turn brown. Soak them in water as soon as you take them out of the food processor and add a few drops of lemon/lime juice or white vinegar.

<u>*Tip for party hosts*</u>: *Grating 10 lbs. of potatoes is time consuming, even with a food processor. If you want to prepare ahead, you can follow the instructions above and soak them in water. Or if you have a food vacuum sealer, you can vacuum seal the shredded potatoes after wringing out the water. That is a better option.*

3. Wringing out the water before mixing the potatoes with flour and eggs is a critical step. You will need a cheese cloth for this. Wring a handful of shredded potatoes at a time. The potatoes should be as dry as possible. You can repeat the wringing a few times. There can be no water in your latke mix. It can cause dangerous oil splashes when you fry the latkes in hot oil!

4. You can save the liquid that you soaked the potatoes in. After a few minutes, the starch in the liquid will settle to the bottom of the bowl. Pour off the liquid. What's left is the potato starch. You can put the starch back into the potato mixture as binding.

5. Fluffier = Better. The flour and the eggs are not only there to bind the shredded potatoes, but they are also there to make it "fluffy". To enhance the effect, add a dash of baking powder in the mixture and mix it evenly.

6. When mixing the ingredients, the first step is always to combine dry flour, baking powder, and seasoning with the potatoes and onions. Mix well. Let the dry mixture sit for a few minutes, so the flour can absorb the extra moisture in the potatoes and onions. Next, pour the liquid, such as beaten eggs, into it little by little. Mix well before you pour more liquid into the mixture. You can stop adding liquid as soon as the mixture can bind and form lumps.

7. Fry the latkes ASAP. No matter how good a job you thought you did in wringing the water out, shredded potatoes have the magical power of retaining water. More water will eventually come out. That's the other reason why you don't want to put too much liquid into the mixture.

8. If you are using an electric deep fryer, to prevent latkes from sticking to the frying basket, first put the frying basket into the hot oil, then drop the latke patties into the basket. Do not fry too many latkes all at once. Make sure there is enough space in between them so they do not stick together. After 1 minute, use a wooden or metal spatula to check to make sure they are not stuck to the bottom of the frying basket. Unstick patties as necessary with sharp metal spatula. Fry latkes for another minute or until golden brown.

9. You can make potato latkes for your gluten-free friends by substituting regular flour with gluten-free flour. If it's not available, other acceptable substitutes include corn starch, tapioca starch, and rice flour.

10. Make bite size latkes. There are many latkes to savor at your party. Don't let your guests fill up on 3 regular size latkes. Make 2" mini latkes. Your guests will appreciate it.

THE ELECTRIC DEEP FRYER – A HANUKKAH MIRACLE

I decided to write a section just for the electric deep fryer. Invest in a good deep fryer, even if you only use it once a year. It is a game changer. Have you tripped your smoke detector when you try to deep fry something on your stove? Nothing is worse than that when hosting a party. Well, actually, there is one thing that is worse – the greasy smell lingering in your house for days. The electric deep fryer solves these problems. I set up a frying station in the garage and keep the garage door open when cooking (in my beautiful Northern California mild winter home). It is the cleanest operation. The other advantage an electric fryer has over the traditional frying pan is consistency in temperature. It is very hard to control the temperature in your frying pan. Usually in the beginning, the temperature is too low. Your latkes soak up a bunch of oil, but the color doesn't turn golden brown. After a batch or two, your frying pan gets too hot and the latkes turn black as soon as you drop them in the pan. An electric fryer will reach the temperature you need and stay at that temperature – a guarantee that your latkes will come out perfectly golden brown and crispy every time.

You may be thinking "But how about all that oil? To submerge all the latkes, don't you need a lot of oil? If the latkes soak up all that oil, it can't be good for my cholesterol." Not true. Submerging your food in hot oil will result in less oil in your food. I know this is counterintuitive. A deep fryer cooks the food by putting high temperature in direct contact with your food, not by the hot oil getting in your food. Before oil gets into your food, the food is already cooked by the heat. For example, at 360°F, latkes can turn golden brown and be perfectly cooked in about 2 minutes. The oil level in the fryer will hardly drop. At one party, I probably fried over 100 latkes without adding a single drop of oil to the deep fryer because not much oil had been absorbed. I figured at this rate, I could fry latkes for 8 days with the oil that is only supposed to last one in a traditional pan over the stove. That's what I call a Hanukkah miracle!

Chapter 2 – The Unusual Latke Recipes

Now we are getting into what this book is about. You will find 16 different latke recipes in this section. There are many ways to add "all that jazz" to the traditional latke recipe. But in general, they fall under the following categories:

1. Change the main ingredient. Examples include:

    Silky Taro Latke (Page 29)
    Butternut Squash Latke and Winter Spice (Page 11)
    Lotus Root and Ginger Latke (Page 23)

2. Add other ingredients into the mix. Examples include:

    Thai Curry Latke (Page 35)
    Pad Thai Latke (Page 25)
    Haggis Latke (Page 19)
    Sticky Rice Flour Latke (Page 31)
    Coconut Sweet Potato Latke (Page 15)
    Deep Fried Banana Latke (Page 17)

3. Add fancy "toppings" on the latke. Examples include:

    Sushi Latke (Page 33)
    Peking Duck Latke (Page 27)
    Baked Brie Latke (Page 9)
    Caprese Latke (Page 13)
    Honey Walnut Sea Bass Latke (Page 21)

4. Layer the latke. Example:

    Baaa-Lapeño Latke (Page 7)

5. A hybrid of all the above. Example:

    Coconut S'mores Latke (Page 15)

You can use different root vegetables. Potato is a root vegetable. So are taro, sweet potato, carrots, lotus roots, etc. Virtually all root vegetables with a low water content can be used for the basic ingredient of latkes. Low water content is the key. So no daikon or radishes. In fact, some non-root vegetables or even fruits can work so long as they are "dry". You will also notice the difference in starch content among these different vegetables. For example, beets and carrots have very little starch and thus you need more flour to "glue" them together.

BAAA-LAPEÑO LATKE

Makes 36 2" mini latkes

(Courtesy of Amanda and Jeremy Fox)

All ingredients in the Classic Potato Latke recipe

For the filling

- 1 lb ground lamb
- 1 white onion, finely diced
- 2 garlic cloves, minced
- 1 or 2 finely minced jalapeño peppers or red chili peppers
- Salt and pepper to taste

1. Prepare Classic Potato Latke mix.
2. Prepare the filling
    i. In a pan with 1 tbsp oil, cook finely diced onions until brown.
    ii. Add garlic and jalapeño peppers (or red chili peppers) into the pan. Cook until fragrant.
    iii. Mix cooked onion, garlic and peppers with ground lamb.
3. Spoon about 1 tbsp of meat filling into the center of the potato mixture.
4. Cover it with another layer of the potato mixture. Then you have meat filled latkes!
5. Fry the meat filled latkes until golden brown (a minute or two longer than regular unfilled latkes).
6. Garnish with slices of jalapeño or red chili peppers.
7. Serve hot.

This recipe is ingenious. The lamb filled center is a total surprise. The kick at the end adds additional layers and depth to this recipe. Also, worth mentioning is that Amanda and Jeremy raise sheep on their property. The success of this recipe also benefits from the grass-fed lamb that were raised with care in the beautiful California weather.

Drink Pairing
A full-bodied or medium-bodied Cabernet Sauvignon or Syrah
A Riesling with medium to low acidity

BAKED BRIE LATKE

Makes 36 2" mini latkes

All ingredients in the Classic Potato Latke recipe

2 round brie wheels, each cut into 18 wedges
Honey
(Optional) 18 fresh figs

1. Prepare potato latkes (see "Classic Potato Latke" recipe).
2. (Optional) Cut figs into halves.
3. Place the latkes on a greased baking sheet. Top a piece of brie on each latke. If you have figs, stack a fig half on top of the brie.
4. Preheat oven to 400°F.
5. Bake until brie melts and figs are warm, about 5 minutes.
6. Drizzle with honey.
7. Serve immediately.

You can't go wrong with baked brie with a hint of sweetness...

Drink Pairing
An old-world style white wine

Substitution
You can substitute figs with fresh or dry fruits or fruit jams. If you use dry fruits or fruit jam, add fruits or jam after baking the latkes and brie, right before serving.

BUTTERNUT SQUASH AND WINTER SPICE LATKE

Makes 36 2" mini latkes

2 lbs butternut squash, peeled
2 medium size onions, finely chopped
3 large eggs, beaten
1 cup all-purpose flour
1 tsp table salt

2 tsp baking powder
1 tsp black pepper
4 tbsp brown sugar
1 tsp cinnamon
1 tsp nutmeg
Oil for frying

Needless to say, this one smells and tastes like the holidays…

Drink Pairing
Mulled wine
Sangria
Hot hard cider

1. Hand grate butternut squash with a box grater or cut butternut squash into cubes and use a food processor with a coarse grating disk to grate the cubes.
2. Combine finely chopped onions and shredded butternut squashes.
3. Wring out as much water as possible in the butternut squashes and onions.
4. Add all dry ingredients (flour, salt, baking powder, black pepper, brown sugar, cinnamon, nutmeg) to the mixture and mix well.
5. Slowly pour in liquids (beaten eggs). Mix as you pour in the eggs. Stop adding eggs as soon as all ingredients are well bound and can form lumps.
6. Put a heaping spoonful of the mixture into your hands and form into patties.
7. Fry the patties until golden brown.
8. Serve hot.

CAPRESE LATKE

Makes 36 2" mini latkes

All ingredients in the Classic Potato Latke recipe

16 oz fresh mozzarella balls, sliced	**1 tsp dried basil**
4 medium heirloom tomatoes	**1 tsp fresh pepper**
8 oz fresh basil leaves	**2 tbsp extra virgin**
1 tsp oregano	**Olive oil for drizzling**
1 tsp fennel seeds	**Oil for frying**

1. Prepare potato latkes mix (see "Classic Potato Latke" recipe).
2. In the mix, add oregano, fennel seeds, dried basil. Let the mixture sit for 15 minutes to allow the flavor of dried spices to be absorbed in the mixture.
3. Fry the latkes until golden brown as in classic potato latke.
4. Top latke with a slice of mozzarella, then a slice of tomato, and finally a basil leaf.
5. Sprinkle with fresh pepper. Drizzle with extra virgin olive oil.
6. Serve immediately (before the juice from the tomatoes gets into the latke and makes it soggy).

The tomatoes and basil leaves give so much freshness to the latke. It's a perfect appetizer.

Drink Pairing
A medium or light-bodied Sangiovese or Zinfandel
A medium or light-bodied Chardonnay or Viognier

COCONUT SWEET POTATO LATKE

Makes 36 2" mini latkes

2 lbs sweet potatoes, peeled
1 cup sweetened coconut flakes
3/4 cup silvered almonds
3 large eggs, beaten

1 cup all-purpose flour
1/2 tsp table salt
2 tsp baking powder
Oil for frying

Who said latkes have to be savory? Latkes can make an excellent dessert!

Drink Pairing
A dark stout or port
Hot Pu-er tea

Tip
You will notice sweet potatoes are drier than potatoes and have less starch. Therefore, you won't wring out as much liquid.

1. Hand grate sweet potatoes with a box grater or use a food processor with a coarse grating disk, similar to the process of making classic potato latkes.
2. Add dry flour, coconut flakes, silvered almonds, salt, and baking powder. Mix well. Slowly add eggs. Mix well as you pour in the eggs. Stop adding eggs as soon as desired consistency is achieved.
3. Fry the latkes the same way as classic potato latkes.
4. Serve immediately.

COCONUT S'MORES LATKE

Additional ingredients
1/2 cup mini marshmallows   12 oz chocolate chips

1. Preheat oven. Use broil setting.
2. Top freshly fried coconut sweet potato latkes with mini marshmallows and chocolate chips. Place on baking sheet.
3. Broil for 1 min in the oven until chocolate chips are slightly melted and marshmallows are slightly roasted. Or preheat oven to 400°F and bake for 3 minutes.
4. Serve immediately.

DEEP FRIED BANANA LATKE Makes 36 2" mini latkes

2 lbs sweet potatoes, peeled
4 medium bananas
1 tsp cinnamon
2 tsp honey
Oil for frying
(Optional) Whipped cream

This is a naturally gluten-free recipe and a perfect dessert.

Drink Pairing
Mai Tai
Piña colada
Vanilla rum on ice

1. Grate sweet potatoes by hand or with a food processor. Wring out liquid as with classic potato latkes.
2. Mash bananas.
3. Combine mashed bananas, honey, and cinnamon. Mix well.
4. Add mixture to shredded and dried sweet potatoes. Mix well.
5. Form the mix into lumps/patties, and fry in hot oil until golden brown. Close the lid when frying and be careful of possible splashes in hot oil because there is more moisture in the mixture than other recipes in this book. The latkes will come out a little softer than normal flour-bound latkes. Be careful when you take them out of the frying basket.
6. Serve hot. Whipped cream is optional.

HAGGIS LATKE

Makes 48 2" mini latkes

All ingredients in the Classic Potato Latke recipe

For Haggis

- 8 tbsp olive oil
- 2 small onions, finely diced
- 2 tsp salt
- 1 tsp ground black pepper
- 2 tsp ground coriander
- 2 tsp nutmeg
- 2 tsp allspice
- 1 tsp dried thyme or fresh, slightly chopped if fresh
- 1/2 tsp cinnamon
- 2 lbs ground or minced lamb
- 2 cups salted chicken or beef stock
- 8 oz oatmeal

1. Prepare Haggis:
    i. Preheat oven to 350°F.
    ii. Heat up olive oil in a pan. Cook onions in oil at medium heat until softened.
    iii. Add salt and spices and thyme to the onions and cook for one minute.
    iv. Add lamb.
    v. Brown meat then when all cooked, add chicken or beef stock and cover. Allow to simmer for around 20 minutes.
    vi. Add oatmeal, mix well and transfer to an oven dish.
    vii. Cover the dish and put in the oven for 30 minutes.
    viii. Remove the lid and cook another 10 minutes until liquid is completely absorbed by oatmeal.
2. Prepare latke mix as in classic potato latkes.
3. Mix potato latke mix with haggis.
4. Form the mix into patties. The patties should be larger and taller than the bite-sized ones in the rest of this recipe book. The patty should be well formed to avoid losing its form in hot oil.
5. Fry haggis latke patties until golden brown.
6. Serve hot.

Jeff and I went to Scotland in 2018. We fell in love with Scotland, as well as its "national food" - Haggis. Jeff's mother is of Scottish ancestry and a part of the Gunn clan. This recipe is a perfect blend of comfort food of two cultures. Traditionally, haggis is made from lamb heart, lungs and often liver in lamb stomach. They are not readily available in grocery stores in many parts of the world. In this recipe, we simplify it by using minced/ground lamb. If you have trouble finding it, substituting with ground beef is just fine.

Drink Pairing
A Scottish Ale or Russian Imperial Stout

HONEY WALNUT SEA BASS LATKE

Makes 36 2" mini latkes

All ingredients in the Classic Potato Latke recipe

2 lbs thick sea bass filet, cut into 1" to 2" chunks
1 cup candied walnut halves
1 tsp salt
1 cup mochiko (glutinous rice flour)
3/4 cup egg whites

For Honey Sauce:
4 tbsp honey
2 tbsp mayonnaise
2 tbsp sweetened condensed milk

1. Prepare potato latkes (see "Classic Potato Latke" recipe).
2. Whip egg whites until foamy. Stir in the mochiko and salt until it has a pasty consistency.
3. Heat the oil in a heavy deep skillet over medium-high heat. Dip sea bass chunks into the mochiko batter, and then fry in the hot oil until golden brown, about 3 minutes. Remove with a slotted spoon and drain on paper towels.
4. Prepare Honey Sauce: In a medium size bowl, stir together mayonnaise, honey, and sweetened condensed milk.
5. Toss sea bass chunks in Honey Sauce.
6. Top each latke with 1 sea bass chunk and then 1 candied walnut.
7. Drizzle with extra Honey Sauce.
8. Serve immediately.

Honey Walnut Shrimp is probably among the most popular Chinese dishes in America. I substituted shrimp with sea bass to make it kosher. The mild flavor of sea bass achieves similar results as compared to shrimp, if not better. You can also use other ingredients such as tofu and chicken, or even crispy fruits and veggies such as water chestnuts or apples.

Drink Pairing
A medium or full-bodied buttery Chardonnay

LOTUS ROOT AND GINGER LATKE

Makes 36 2" mini latkes

- 2 lbs lotus roots, peeled
- 2 medium size onions, finely chopped
- 3 large eggs, beaten
- 1 cup all-purpose flour
- 2 tsp table salt
- 2 tsp baking powder
- 1 tsp black pepper
- 2 tsp grated ginger
- Oil for frying
- (Optional) ponzu sauce

1. Hand grate lotus roots with a box grater or cut lotus roots into cubes and use a food processor with a coarse grating disk to grate the cubes.
2. Combine finely chopped onions and shredded lotus roots.
3. Wring out as much water as possible in the lotus roots and onions.
4. Add all dry ingredients (flour, salt, baking powder, black pepper) to the mixture and mix well.
5. Slowly pour in liquids (beaten eggs). Mix as you pour in the eggs. Stop adding eggs as soon as all ingredients are well bound and can form lumps.
6. Add grated ginger and mix well.
7. Put a heaping spoonful of the mixture into your hands and form into patties.
8. Fry the patties as classic potato latkes. Do not overcook it. Otherwise it will lose the crunchiness.
9. Serve hot with ponzu sauce.

I remember that one of the traditional dishes in my hometown, Tianjin, is deep fried lotus roots. Lotus roots are cut into slices, coated with batter, and dropped into the frying pan. I loved the crunchy lotus roots even when fully cooked. You will find the slight crunchiness in the texture of this lotus root latke very interesting.

Drink Pairing
A cold filtered sake

PAD THAI LATKE

Makes 36 2" mini latkes

All ingredients in the Classic Potato Latke recipe. Cut quantity by half.

2 cups leftover Pad Thai noodles

1. Combine all classic potato latke ingredients to make potato latke mix.
2. Coarsely chop the Pad Thai noodles into 1" long sections.
3. Combine latke mix with Pad Thai. Mix well.
4. Fry Pad Thai latke in hot oil until golden brown.
5. Garnish with green onions, extra peanuts, cilantro or lime wedges.
6. Serve immediately. Use extra Pad Thai sauce for dipping.

This is very easy if you have leftover Pad Thai. But if you don't, you can make Pad Thai from scratch. See below for a good Pad Thai recipe.

Drink Pairing
An aromatic Gewurztraminer or Riesling

PAD THAI NOODLES

Makes 2 cups

8 ounces flat rice noodles
3 tbsp oil
3 cloves garlic, minced
2 eggs, beaten
1/2 cup fresh bean sprouts
1 red bell pepper, thinly sliced
3 green onions, chopped
1/2 cup dry roasted peanuts
2 limes

For Pad Thai sauce:
3 tbsp fish sauce
1 tbsp low-sodium soy sauce
5 tbsp light brown sugar
2 tbsp rice vinegar
1 tbsp Sriracha hot sauce, or to taste

1. Cook noodles according to package instructions or until tender. Rinse under cold water.
2. Mix the all Pad Thai sauce ingredients together. Set aside.
3. Heat 1 1/2 tbsp of oil in a large saucepan or wok over medium-high heat.
4. Add garlic, onions, and bell pepper. Cook for about 2 minutes.
5. Push everything to the side of the pan. Add a little more oil and add the beaten eggs. Scramble the eggs, breaking them into small pieces with a spatula as they cook.
6. Add cooked noodles, sauce, bean sprouts and peanuts to the pan. Toss everything to combine.
7. Set aside to cool off.

PEKING DUCK LATKE

Makes 36 2" mini latkes

All ingredients in the Classic Potato Latke recipe

10 oz Peking duck with crispy skin
3 tbsp Chinese sweet flour sauce AKA Chinese sweet bean sauce,
or
3 tbsp Hoisin sauce,
or
3 tbsp Chinese black bean sauce

4 green onions, sliced into very thin strips
1 cucumber, peeled, cut into very thin strips
(Optional) 1 wedge of cantaloupe, peeled and cut into very thin strips

Being a Chinese Jewish American woman, Peking duck has a special place in my heart (and my stomach)…

Drink Pairing
A full-bodied or medium-bodied Cabernet Sauvignon
A slightly smoky Syrah or Pinot Noir

1. Prepare potato latkes (see "Classic Potato Latke" recipe).
2. Slice the Peking duck into thin slices. Make sure each slice is covered with some crispy skin. For best results, get it sliced by the professionals in the restaurant. (Normally, you buy Peking duck in a local Chinese restaurant.)
3. Spread a small amount of Chinese sweet flour sauce on top of the freshly fried latkes, then stack a slice of duck on top.

   If you do not have Chinese sweet flour sauce, there are two ways to make something similar in taste:
   a. Use Hoisin sauce as base. Hoisin sauce is sweeter than sweet flour sauce. Thus, add some salt or soy sauce to taste. Or,
   b. Use Chinese black bean sauce as base. However, Chinese black bean sauce has the opposite problem. It's too salty and not sweet at all. Thus, add sugar to taste for optimal sweetness.
4. Garnish with green onion strips, cucumber strips, and cantaloupe strips.
5. Serve hot.

Substitution
You can substitute Peking duck with Cantonese roasted duck. Cantonese roasted duck is usually available in the café/deli section in Chinese markets such as 99 Ranch Market. Do not chop it into chunks. Buy it whole and reheat it in an oven at 400°F for 10 minutes to make the skin crispy. Then slice the breast. Again, make sure each slice is covered with some crispy skin.

SILKY TARO LATKE

(Courtesy of Matt Schlachtman)

Makes 36 2" mini latkes

1 large taro root or many small ones, about 2 lbs
2 large shallots or onions
2 large eggs, beaten
2 tsp salt
1 tsp pepper
Oil for frying

For dipping sauce:
1 cup of sour cream or plain Greek yogurt
1 tbsp of lime juice
1/4 cup sriracha
2 finely chopped Persian cucumbers
2 tbsp dill

You will notice taro is an excellent root vegetable for latkes, as it has a lot of natural starch. Taro starch differs from potato starch in that it's creamy. This creaminess eliminates the need to use extra flour as a binding agent and also gives the latkes a unique silky mouth feel. This is also an excellent gluten-free recipe.

Drink Pairing
A crisp Sauvignon Blanc or Pinot Grigio with higher acidity

1. Peel taro skin (be careful the flesh is very slimy and slippery).
2. Hand grate taro or use grating attachment on a food processor.
3. Dab dry taro with paper towels or clean cloth to remove moisture, but do not wring, and place in fridge to rest for 10-15 minutes.
4. Mince shallots or onions.
5. With small amount of oil lightly sauté minced shallots, until fragrant, but not browned.
6. In a bowl, mix taro, eggs, shallots, and salt and pepper.
7. Form the latke patties and fry in hot oil until golden brown.
8. Mix all dipping sauce ingredients to make dipping sauce.
9. Serve silky taro latkes hot with dipping sauce.

STICKY RICE FLOUR LATKE

Makes 36 2" mini latkes

2 lbs potatoes peeled
2 medium size onions
1 cup egg whites
1 cup rice flour
2 tsp table salt
1 tsp baking powder
1 tsp black pepper
Oil for frying

(Optional) Honey Sauce
 4 tbsp honey
 2 tbsp mayonnaise
 2 tbsp sweetened condensed milk
(Optional) apple sauce
(Optional) sour cream

This recipe is gluten-free. It's also very soft and fluffy.

Drink Pairing
An unfiltered sake
An aromatic Gewurztraminer or Riesling

1. Grate potatoes and onions. Wring out liquid as with classic potato latke. Add salt and black pepper. Mix well.
2. Combine baking powder and rice flour. Mix well.
3. Beat egg whites until foamy. Fold in rice flour and baking powder.
4. Add the mixture into dry potatoes and onions mixture, little by little, until desired consistency is achieved.
5. Fry the latkes until golden brown.
6. Drizzle honey sauce on top and serve hot. Or serve with apple sauce and sour cream.

SUSHI LATKE   Makes 36 2" mini latkes

All ingredients in the Classic Potato Latke recipe

10 oz assorted sashimi
6 oz seaweed salad
6 oz salmon roe
Soy sauce or ponzu sauce for dipping
(Optional) Lemon peel or chives as garnish

For Miso Dressing
1 tbsp lemon juice
1/2 tsp wasabi paste
1 tsp sesame seed oil
1 tbsp miso paste
1 tbsp mayonnaise

This recipe is one of our earliest creations. It's simple and delicious, not to mention beautiful and photogenic.

Drink Pairing
An unfiltered sake
A crisp Sauvignon Blanc or Rose

1. Prepare miso dressing by combining miso paste, mayonnaise, lemon juice, wasabi paste, 1/2 tsp sesame seed oil and mix well.
2. Let mixture stand in refrigerator for 30 minutes.
3. Prepare dipping sauce by mixing remaining sesame seed oil with soy sauce or ponzu sauce.
4. Prepare potato latkes (see "Classic Potato Latke" recipe).
5. Spread small amount of miso dressing on top of the freshly fried latke, top with sashimi, salmon roe or seaweed salad.
6. Garnish with lemon peel or chives.
7. Serve with dipping sauce.

THAI CURRY LATKE

Makes 36 2" mini latkes

2 lbs sweet potatoes, peeled
2 small onions
2 large eggs, beaten
1 cup all-purpose flour
2 tsp baking powder
1 1/2 tsp table salt
1 tsp black pepper
2 tbsp Thai red curry (add more if you like spicy)
2 tbsp curry powder, dissolve in 3 tbsp of water

Oil for frying
2 tbsp coconut oil
(Optional) Dipping Sauce
    2 tbsp creamy peanut butter
    1/4 cup soy sauce
    1/2 cup water

This is another one of my all-time favorites. The subtle sweetness of sweet potatoes blends very well with the curry flavor. And the "kick" from the Thai red curry will have you craving for more…

Drink Pairing
A cold lager or Kolsch beer

Tip
You will notice sweet potatoes are drier than potatoes and have less starch. So you won't wring out as much liquid.

1. Hand grate sweet potatoes and onions with a box grater or use a food processor with a coarse grating disk, like the process of making classic potato latkes.
2. Add flour, salt, baking powder, and black pepper to above ingredients and mix well. In a separate bowl, combine beaten eggs, Thai red curry, and curry powder mixture. Add liquid to the mixture little by little until it is even and well bound. Make sure there are no lumps of Thai curry or curry powder.
3. Fry the latkes the same way as the classic potato latkes.
4. (Optional) Make peanut sauce: Combine peanut butter, soy sauce, and water. Mix well.
5. Serve latkes hot with peanut sauce.

Bonus Recipes – Meatzaballs, Cheetzaballs, and Pizzaballs

BASIC MATZO BALL SOUP RECIPE   Makes 9 matzo balls

1/2 cup matzo meal
2 eggs, beaten
1/4 cup oil
1/2 tsp baking powder
1/2 tsp baking soda

1 tsp salt
1/2 tsp pepper
6 cups water
2 tsp "Better than Bouillon" chicken base

Prepare matzo ball mix
1. Mix dry ingredients into a bowl.
2. Mix oil into beaten eggs.
3. Pour egg mixture into the dry mixture and gently mix with a fork. DO NOT OVER MIX. If you over mix, the mixture will get hard and lose fluffiness.
4. Chill in the refrigerator for 30 min to 1 hour.

Make soup base and cook the matzo balls
5. Boil the water and dissolve the "Better than Bouillon" chicken base.
6. Boil matzo balls in medium heat until the matzo balls float to the top. Then reduce the heat and simmer for 30 to 40 minutes.
7. Serve hot.

Matzo ball soup is great. The tenderness and juiciness you get once you bite into a matzo ball offers so much satisfaction and comfort. It's unbelievable. But sometimes, I wish there were a little something in there to surprise me…

The process of making Meatzaballs, Cheetzaballs, and Pizzaballs is very similar. Basically, we fill matzo balls with different types of filling before boiling. So follow the recipe on this page and make the matzo "wrapper". In the next few pages, you will find the steps on how to make the filling and how to stuff the matzo wrapper. Place the stuffed matzo balls on a well-greased plate or flat surface, so the matzo does not stick to it. (See photo on the opposite page. Then, come back to this page to find how to make the soup and boil the stuffed matzo balls!

FILLING FOR MEATZABALLS

Makes filling for 9 Meatzaballs

1/4 lb ground beef or ground turkey
1 egg, beaten
1 tsp corn starch
1/2 tsp salt
1/2 tsp pepper
1/2 tsp oregano

Prepare Meatzaball filling
1. Combine all filling ingredients. Mix well.
2. Chill in refrigerator for 15 min to let the flavor soak in.

Stuff the matzo wrapper with filling
3. Scoop one 1 tbsp of matzo ball mix into your palm and make it into a ball.
4. Press the center and make a dent in the ball, but do not break the matzo wrapper.
5. a. Put a small amount of meat filling in the wrapper.
   b. Slowly mold the matzo wrapper to cover the entire filling. Make it round with your hand again.
6. Place the stuffed matzo balls on a well-greased plate or flat surface, so the matzo does not stick to it.

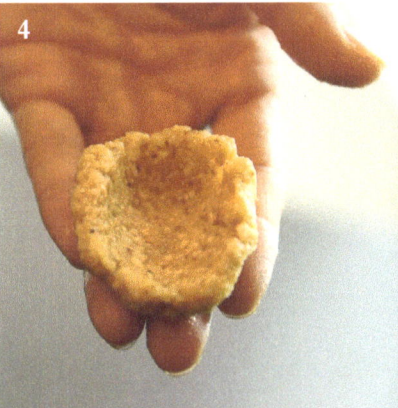

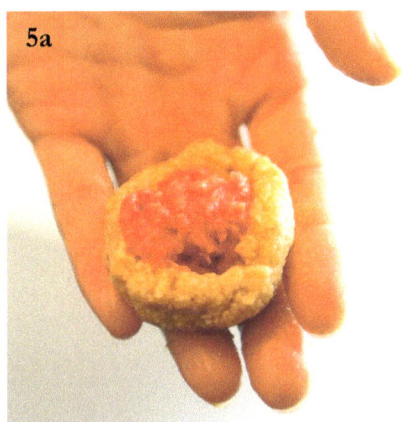

FILLING FOR CHEETZABALLS

Makes filling for 9 Cheetzaballs

4 oz of hard or semi-hard cheese with a strong flavor, i.e. cheddar, gouda, etc.

Prepare Cheetzaball filling
1. Cut cheese into 1/2" cubes

Stuff the matzo wrapper with filling
2. Scoop one 1 tbsp of matzo ball mix into your palm and make it into a ball.
3. Press the center and make a dent in the ball, but do not break the matzo wrapper.
4. a. Place a cheese cube in the wrapper. b. Slowly mold the matzo wrapper to cover the entire filling. Make it round with your hand again. Make sure the filling is completely covered.
5. Place the stuffed matzo balls on a well-greased plate or flat surface, so the matzo does not stick to it.

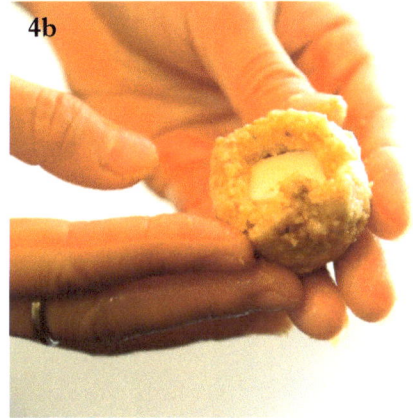

5    8a    8b

FILLING FOR PIZZABALLS

Makes filling for 9 Pizzaballs

You need a small round ice cube mold (i.e. Hutzler 324 Ball Ice Tray 1" in diameter). Make the filling 24 hours ahead and freeze.

1 can of pizza sauce or marinara sauce   4 oz cream cheese

Prepare Pizzaball filling:
1. Cut cream cheese into 3/8" cubes.
2. Place 1 cream cheese cube into each round mold.
3. Spoon pizza sauce or marinara sauce into ice tray.
4. Close the mold and freeze for 24 hours. Overfill the sauce in the ice tray so when you close the mold, each ball is filled with the sauce to the top. Excess sauce will come out of the hole on top of the mold.
5. Take the tray out of the freezer and use the filling immediately.

Stuff the matzo wrapper with filling
6. Scoop one 1 tbsp of matzo ball mix into your palm and make it into a ball.
7. Press the center and make a dent in the ball, but do not break the matzo wrapper.
8. a. Put a frozen pizza sauce "ice ball" in the wrapper.
   b. Slowly mold the matzo wrapper to cover the entire filling. Make it round with your hand again. Make sure the filling is completely covered.
9. Place the stuffed matzo balls on a well-greased plate or flat surface, so the matzo does not stick to it.

Tips
Try to boil the stuffed Pizzaballs as soon as you stuff them. (Preferably drop them in boiling stock as you stuff them.) If left sitting out for too long, the stuffing will melt which makes it hard to pick up the ball.

Serve with no soup or with little soup to prevent the filling from being diluted.

BONUS RECIPE – SCHLACHT-FUDGE
(Courtesy of Matt Schlachtman)

3 cups sugar
3/4 cup butter
1 can (12oz) evaporated milk
(one large can)
(Do not use condensed milk)

1 package (12oz) of semi-sweet chocolate chips
1 10 oz bag of mini marshmallows
(Optional) 1 cup chopped walnuts or pecans
1 tsp. vanilla

1. Grease a 13" X 9" baking pan. Set aside. (Use PAN or lightly brush with butter.) Bring sugar, butter and evaporated milk to full rolling boil in at least a 3-qt. saucepan on medium heat, stirring constantly. Cook at boiling temperature for at least 4 minutes or until candy thermometer reaches 234°F, stirring constantly.
2. Before candy has reached this temperature, microwave marshmallows in a nonstick and microwave safe bowl at continuous increments of 15 seconds until marshmallows start to puff up and are about 1.5-2 times in size.
3. When candy is at 234°F, lower heat to low or simmer.
4. Add chocolate chips and marshmallows; stir THOROUGHLY until all bits of both are fully melted, add nuts (optional) and vanilla. Mix well.
5. Pour into prepared pan; spread to cover bottom of pan. Cool completely at room temperature. Cut into approximately 2" squares or desired blocks.

Over the years, Matt has been solely responsible for the dessert course of our unusual latke parties. In the spirit of being "unusual", Matt not only perfected his fudge making, but also infused his fudge with boundless creativity. He would create a list of new flavors and conduct an online poll among friends and pick the top 3 popular ones to make for that year. Some of them deserve to be recorded in the hall of fame of fudge. Here's the basic recipe. Feel free to build upon it, create your flavors and experiment with the recipes. Have fun!

www.ingramcontent.com/pod-product-compliance
Lightning Source LLC
Chambersburg PA
CBHW041153290426
44108CB00002B/56